Literacy in Action

Building a Community of Readers

A Research-Based Approach to Improving Literacy
Featuring the Schoolwide, Inc. Student-Run Bookstore

Michelle Wolf and Rory Cohen

Grades K-1

Teacher Resource Book

SCHOOLWIDE, INC.
LITERACY PROGRAMS

Scientific research suggests that access to quality literature, rigorous instructional practice and parent/community involvement are critical factors in dramatically improving reading achievement. Literacy in Action is a comprehensive program based on such research. Literacy in Action has three primary components: The Student-Run Bookstore, Classroom Libraries & Teacher's Guides. The bookstore and the libraries provide access to quality literature while the guides instruct teachers on implementing a rigorous reading curriculum that includes home-school connections.

Michelle Wolf and Rory Cohen

Table of Contents

unit 1

Building a Community of Readers

Introduction

Sharing books with students at the emergent literacy stage is a great joy and is one of the most important aspects of teaching K–1 students. Since you read to and with your students every day, you have many opportunities to fire your students' interest and enthusiasm for books as well as their desire to learn to read.

By surrounding your students with books, the Schoolwide Bookstore is one way to help you fuel that fire. Through the Schoolwide Bookstore, your students will have the opportunity to browse through books—just as adults do in bookstores. As they browse, they will pick up and put down many different books, discovering the vast array of books available to them. They will talk about these books with their classmates and share their opinions.

An important goal of the Schoolwide Bookstore is for each of your students to become an active member in a community of readers. If students feel the excitement of being a part of a dynamic book-loving group, they will readily join in. The lessons in Unit 1 will support students in establishing positive reading behaviors and reading readiness skills. They will help you create this exciting community of readers in your classroom and throughout your school by:

• encouraging students to think about and share their attitudes about reading.
• teaching students how to talk about reading with each other and learn more about each community member.
• showing how books are special and can be landmarks in their lives.
• discussing how reading makes each of us grow and learn.
• learning about the tools of reading and how to use them.
• teaching students to learn to recommend books to others.
• allowing students to formulate class rules for independent reading time.
• setting goals for each student to grow as a reader.

Also essential to the success of building a community of readers in your school is parent involvement. To become successful readers, students must read for pleasure both in and outside school. At no age is this more important than in kindergarten and first grade. Through *Home Connections*, which you will find in each unit, the Schoolwide Bookstore has built in many ways for parents to join the community of readers and to build with their child that special bond that comes from sharing and reading together.

Lesson 1
Reading Survey

(1 day) ★

You will need:

- chart paper.
- one copy of *Reading Survey* (BLM 1 and 2, page 7 and 8) for each child.
- markers, crayons, or colored pencils for each child.
- one copy of *Letter to Parents* (BLM 3, page 9) for each child.

Lesson Objective

Lesson 1 will help you introduce the concept of a community of readers and allow you and your students to discover each other's views about reading. Specifically in this lesson you will:

- discuss the concept of a community of readers.
- help students complete the *Reading Survey.*
- encourage students to share survey responses with classmates and families.

★ ★

Mini-Lesson

Write the words *Community of Readers* on the chalkboard or chart paper. Explain to the class that the word community can mean a group of people who all live in one place or area. For example, your neighborhood is a community as is everyone in your school. But a community can also be a group of people who are interested in the same things or share a hobby. Ask students what clubs and communities they belong to. Answers might include sports teams, dance groups, Cub Scouts, church choirs, etc. Discuss what these groups do and what the members share in common.

Explain that the class is a community—a community of *learners.* Discuss with students that a benefit of being part of this community is they will discover and learn many new things. They will learn about new places, people, and other things. Explain that for the next few weeks, the class will be talking a lot about reading and ways to build a strong reading community.

Introduce the *Reading Survey* by telling the class that one way to build a community of readers is to share reading interests and behaviors with each other. Explain that over the next few days the class will be sharing their tastes, interests, and feelings about reading by taking surveys and talking with themselves and their peers.

Tell students that during independent work time today they will receive a reading survey. Model how students will use the survey by completing one on your own. Go over each question slowly and share your answers while you demonstrate how to complete the survey.

▶ Lesson 1
Reading Survey
(1 day) ★

Before distributing copies of the survey, tell students you will read aloud each question so they can fill in their own answers. Distribute copies of the survey to the class and tell students to return to their independent work areas.

Independent Work Time

Once students have their surveys and are ready to begin, slowly read each question aloud. Give students plenty of time to complete their answers.

Share

After students finish their surveys, invite them to the meeting area to share their answers and their drawings with partners or in small groups. After sharing in small groups, read select survey questions aloud and ask students to share their answers with the entire class.

Home Connection

After looking over all the surveys, send each student home with their own survey along with the *Letter to Parents* that accompanies this unit.

Name

_____

- -

_____

Reading Survey
Circle the face that shows how you feel.

1. How do you feel about reading at home?

2. How do you feel about reading at school?

3. How do you feel about spending your free time reading?

4. How do you feel about rereading favorite books?

5. How do you feel about going to the school bookstore?

6. How do you feel about reading aloud?

Name

_____

- -

_____

Reading Survey (Cont.)

7. Draw a picture of yourself reading.

Lesson 1
Reading Survey BLM 3
(1 day) ★

Dear Parent(s) or Guardian(s),

As you may know, we have established a school bookstore that is run by our students. During school, your child will regularly visit the bookstore to choose and purchase books. This will enable your child to build a home library of books he or she loves. We also encourage you to visit the school bookstore with your child to browse through the many books available.

Why do we have this bookstore? It is important to surround students with great books and get them excited about reading. At kindergarten and first grade, it is critical that students read and are read to daily. This helps them build on their reading skills learned at school. In addition, they will also learn to value reading as an important part of their lives.

Today we are beginning a unit of study called *Building a Community of Readers*. During this unit and throughout the year, we will be celebrating books, talking about books, and reading books. We invite you to join our community of readers and help your child celebrate books by reading together at home.

To start this unit, your child completed a survey to tell us his or her feelings about reading. That survey is attached to this letter. Please read it and talk about it in a positive way with your child. Please understand that there are no right or wrong answers. Use this survey as a starting point to help guide your child to pursue a life-long joy for reading.

Keep this survey in a safe place. You and your child may enjoy looking back at it in a few months, at the end of the year, and in years to come.

If there is anything about your child's reading life that you would like to share with me, write a note on the back of this page. Then, send it to school with your child tomorrow. I would be very interested in learning more about your child's habits and attitudes towards reading.

Thank you for your help and for becoming a member of our community of readers.

Sincerely,

Building a Community of Readers

► Lesson 2
Learning about Other Readers
(2 days) ★

You will need:

• chart paper.

Lesson Objective

Lesson 2 will explore the many ways that students can get to know other members of a community of readers. It will also show students that talking about books is a good way for them to learn more about each other, and that one of the joys of reading comes from sharing books. Specifically in this lesson you will:

• help students brainstorm a list of questions they might ask to get to know each other as readers.
• have students interview classmates and family members.
• have students share something they learned about another reader.

★ ★

Mini-Lesson (day 1)

Discuss how sharing their reading surveys from Lesson 1 helped them get to know more about each other as readers. Explain that they will get to know even more today by interviewing each other. Tell students that one of the best ways to get to know another reader is by talking about books and asking questions.

Show students a chart labeled *Possible Reading Interview Questions*. Tell students that you want them to brainstorm questions about reading that they could ask their peers. Begin by giving a few examples and writing them on the chart paper. For example, "Who is the person you most like to have read to you?" "What is your favorite time to read?" "How many books do you have in your bedroom?"

Once you feel students have a sense of the kinds of questions to ask about reading, have them share their ideas and add their questions to the chart.

Lesson 2
Learning about Other Readers

(2 days) ★

Tell students that during independent reading time today, you want them to interview each other. They should look at the chart if they need question ideas. Your chart might look like the following.

Possible Questions for Other Readers

- What kinds of books do you like?
- What's your favorite book?
- Who do you talk with about books?
- What books made you laugh out loud?
- Do you know any books by heart?
- What time of day or night do you read or get read to most?
- What's the last book you read?
- Who is your favorite author?

Independent Work Time

Have students work with partners or in small groups. Use this time to circulate and support students in asking and answering questions.

Share

Gather students in the meeting area. Tell them you want them to share one thing they learned about another reader in the class. Give each student an opportunity to share at least one thing about another student.

★ ★

▶ Teaching Tip

Kindergarten and first-grade students may have difficulty differentiating between a question and a statement. You should not expect to teach this concept during this lesson. If a student suggests a statement such as "My favorite book is...." rephrase their statement as a question, "Oh, so you think finding out each other's favorite books is a good idea? I agree. Let's write the question, 'What is your favorite book?' on our chart."

Lesson 2
Learning about Other Readers
(2 days) ★

Mini-Lesson (day 2)

Reread the list of questions your class generated in the day 1 mini-lesson. Explain to students that today, they will have an opportunity to interview other students in the class. Tell them that during independent reading time, you want them to interview two new students, and just like yesterday, you want them to ask questions and talk about reading.

Independent Work Time

As students interview each other, be sure to circulate and support students' reading conversations. Take notes on generalities and things that students have in common. Refer to these notes during Share time.

Share

Once students are gathered in the meeting area, begin by having them share something they learned about another reader. Tell them that as you listened, you noticed the reading community has a lot of things in common. Begin a chart titled *Our Reading Community...* On the chart, list things your community has in common. Items for the list should be taken from information gained in Lesson 1 and Lesson 2. Your chart might look like the one on the right.

Our Reading Community. . .

- Has favorite authors.
- Likes to be read to.
- Has favorite books.
- Reads before we go to bed at night.
- Loves to look at pictures in books.
- Likes to read to people.
- Likes to share books with friends.
- Likes books about animals.
- Knows some books by heart.

SCHOOLWIDE, INC.
LITERACY PROGRAMS
12
©2005 Schoolwide, Inc. • **Unit 1** Building a Community of Readers • *Grades K-1*

Lesson 3
Rules and Routines for Independent Reading
(1 day) ★

You will need:

• chart paper and markers.

Lesson Objective

In Lesson 3 students will learn what to do during independent reading time and make a list of rules for this important daily block of time. Specifically in this lesson you will:

• help students create a list of practical rules and routines for independent reading.
• build community by establishing and agreeing to a reading contract.

★ ★

Mini-Lesson

Explain that today, you want to talk about independent reading. Tell students it is important that the class establish rules to follow during this time so that everyone can enjoy reading and work at becoming strong independent readers.

Tell students that today, the class will create a list of rules that they all agree to and form a contract for independent reading time. Explain that a contract is an agreement put in writing and signed by the people involved. By signing the contract, each person agrees to follow the rules.

Have students begin brainstorming a list of rules. Write the suggestions on a piece of chart paper. Moderate the discussion to be sure that the rules are fair and enforceable. Be sure to be involved in the process by suggesting rules you know will be important in creating a strong independent reading time.

After a list of rules has been generated, have students pick the ones that they agree are important and useful. When you and the class are satisfied with the list of rules, write them on a new piece of chart paper, leaving room for the students to sign their names or initials. Tell students to come up to the chart and finalize their contract for independent reading time by signing it. Then, post the contract on a bulletin board. Your rules and routines might include some found on the chart shown on page 14.

Lesson 3
Rules and Routines for Independent Reading

(1 day) ★

Rules for Independent Reading Time

- Pick books you think you'll like and can read.
- Choose a quiet reading nook and stay there for the entire reading time.
- Put books back in the right place so others can find them.
- Big books can only be used in the Read-Along corner.
- Be focused and productive 100% of the time.
- Use headphones to read along silently with taped readings.
- When meeting with the teacher, speak very quietly to not disturb other readers and writers.
- Write your name or initials on the log for the bathroom passes; walk quietly in and out.
- Only get supplies from the correct places so you don't disturb others.
- Keep the classroom quiet and be respectful of each other at all times.
- Remember to use reading tools and to treat books carefully.

Tell students that every day they will have independent reading time. Reiterate that this is a time for them to enjoy reading and work on becoming strong independent readers. Explain that since the class now has a list of rules, you expect that these rules be followed.

Independent Work Time

Invite students to select some books and practice independent reading. During independent reading time in kindergarten and first grade, you should expect to see students looking at books with partners, rereading or retelling favorite books, taking picture walks through books, or looking at pictures in nonfiction texts.

Be sure to return students' attention to the reading contract often during the next few weeks to reinforce the rules and routines established during this lesson.

Lesson 3
Rules and Routines for Independent Reading
(1 day) ★

Share

Bring the class together and have students discuss how their first day of independent reading went and how they could make it better next time.

★ ★

▶ Teaching Tip

Some things on this chart like teaching tools and reading nooks, will be discussed in future lessons. You can put them on your list and tell students you will talk more about them in the future, or you can add them to the list after you have introduced them.

▶ Teaching Tip

Eventually, students in kindergarten and first grade should be able to read independently for 20 to 25 minutes each day. It is a good idea to set this as a goal and work slowly up to it.

It is important for independent reading time to feel productive. The length of your independent reading time should be only as long as students are able to maintain focus and productivity. As you begin, plan a 10-minute independent reading time. Increase this time as you notice your students reading stamina building.

Before moving along to the next group of lessons, it is a good idea to spend a couple of days working on establishing a strong independent reading time. If you decide to do this, use your mini-lesson time to highlight single rules from your reading contract. Mini-lessons can be used to discuss rules and routines, related issues, and solutions.

► Lesson 4
Reasons for Reading
(2 days) ★

You will need:

- chart paper.
- one copy each of *Reasons for Reading Illustrations* (BLMs 4–8, pages 19–25)
- one copy of *Letter to Parents* (BLM 9, page 24) for each child.
- one copy of *My Reading Walk at Home* (BLM 10, page 25) for each child.

Lesson Objective

Lesson 4 will encourage your students to brainstorm the many different types of writing and reading experiences people meet in daily life. This will help them see there are many reasons for reading. Then, you will take them on a "reading walk" to find more of the situations and reasons for which people read, including for work, daily survival, and pleasure. Specifically in this lesson you will:

- show students photos of people reading and discuss the many reasons to read.
- take students on a reading walk to discover more reasons to read.
- have each student do a reading walk at home.

★ ★

Mini-Lesson (day 1)

Write the heading *Reasons for Reading* on the chalkboard or chart paper. Ask students to help you brainstorm a list of reasons why people read. After some reasons have been supplied, show the students the *Reasons for Reading Illustrations* and ask the class to explain what the person is doing and explain what their reason for doing it might be. Use their responses to add to your *Reasons for Reading* list. Your completed chart might look like the following.

Reasons for Reading

- Because it is fun
- It is relaxing
- To spend time with family
- To learn or investigate new things
- For safety (traffic signals)
- To find your way to a new place
- To work machines or computers
- To follow rules
- To find prices
- To learn something new or to look things up in reference books

SCHOOLWIDE, INC.
LITERACY PROGRAMS

Lesson 4
Reasons for Reading
(2 days) ★

After brainstorming ideas for reasons for reading, tell students that before they go into the library today, you want them to think about their reason for selecting a book. Do they want to select a book that will make them laugh? Do they want to select a book that will help them learn about something? Or do they have another reason in mind?

Independent Work Time

Send students to the library to select books for independent reading. As you conference, be sure to talk to students about their reason for selecting their books.

Share

Bring the class back together and ask for volunteers to share what books they found. Ask students why they choose that particular book. If a student mentions a reason for reading not previously discussed, be sure to add it to the *Reasons for Reading* chart.

Mini-Lesson (day 2)

Explain to the class that you are going to take a "reading walk" to see if they can discover more reasons for reading. Tell students they will walk around the school ending up in the student bookstore. Ask students to look for writing and to think about why people might need to read that writing. Model how to do this by looking around the classroom pointing out writing such as a calendar or a lunch menu. Explain the reasons why you would need to read that writing, e.g., to plan your week or month or to decide what to eat. Explain that after the reading walk, the class will add to the list of reasons for reading.

▶ Lesson 4
Reasons for Reading
(2 days) ★

Take a 15 to 20 minute walk through and around the school. Walk through the school office, storerooms, mechanical rooms, and library. Encourage students to point out any printed words that they see and any people they see reading. Read the words aloud for students and talk about their meanings. Finish the walk in the Schoolwide Bookstore and give students time to look around and talk about the different types of writing (prices, posters, etc.) and books they find there.

Share

Upon returning to class, gather students in the meeting area and look at the *Reasons for Reading* chart. Go over the chart and add any new ideas gathered from the walk. Tell students that tonight for homework, you would like them to take a reading walk at home. Explain you will add any new ideas to the class chart that they bring in the next day.

Home Connection

Give each student a copy of *My Reading Walk at Home* and the *Letter to Parents* to take home. Encourage them to discuss with family members what they have already found on their reading walk at school. Model for them how they might use the worksheet to record their findings.

The next day, ask students to share new reasons they found at home, and add these to the class list. Offer suggestions for any additional reasons that students do not mention.

SCHOOLWIDE, INC.
LITERACY PROGRAMS

Dear Parent(s) or Guardian(s),

Today at school our class took a "reading walk." We walked around our school and the school bookstore to find places where we could see written words, signs, and messages. When we found them, we talked about the reasons the writing was there. We came up with a list of the many reasons people read including for fun, to find their way, to learn rules, and so on.

Ask your child to tell you about the reading walk that we took. Ask him or her to describe some of the reasons for reading that we found and all the types of books we found in the student bookstore. Then, take your child on a reading walk in your home or neighborhood. Walk through each room in the house and around the neighborhood to find places where words and writing appear. When you find them, read the words aloud for your child and talk about the meaning and the reasons the words are there. Help your child write the reasons down on the attached sheet and have her or him bring it back to school tomorrow.

Whenever you are out with your child, point out different types of writing you come across. Talk about the reasons it is there. This is one simple way to build your child's enthusiasm for reading.

Thanks again for being a part of our community of readers.

Sincerely,

Building a Community of Readers

Lesson 4
Reasons for Reading BLM 10
(2 days) ★

Name

My Reading Walk at Home
**Write down the writing you find at home and in your neighborhood.
Explain why it is there.**

Kitchen

Living or Family Room

Bedroom

Neighborhood

▶ Lesson 5
Landmark Books
(2 days)★ ★

You will need:

- selected landmark books from your life to share.
- chalkboard or chart paper.
- one copy of *Letter to Parents* (BLM 11, page 29) for each child.

Lesson Objective

Lesson 5 focuses on the important role that books play in our lives and the power of books to enrich and change our lives. Specifically in this lesson you will:

- tell students about books that have been landmarks in your life.
- share these books and their importance.
- ask parents to help their child choose a landmark book to share with the class.
- read aloud and discuss the students' landmark books.
- compile a list of landmark books to share with families.

★ ★

Mini-Lesson (day 1)

Write the word *landmark* on the chalkboard or chart paper. Explain that the word *landmark* has two meanings. Point out a famous landmark in your town or area and explain that famous buildings, tall mountains, bridges, etc. can be landmarks. Landmarks are something you can see and recognize from a distance, helping you know your location. Then, explain that landmark has another meaning. An important event or a major change in a person's life can also be a landmark.

Discuss with the class that certain books are very important to people. Sometimes people read these books so often they know them by heart. Other books remind us of important times in our lives or of a person who is very special to us. For example, some of us have special books that our parents or grandparents always read to us. These special books can change our lives by what we learn when we read them. These books can become landmarks in our lives.

Tell students that you are going to share some of your landmark books. Show them the covers and tell a little about each book. Share why each book is a landmark to you. You might select a book you remember reading as a child, a book you read on a vacation, a book that reminds you of a special person or time, or a book that introduced you to a new and favorite author.

Lesson 5
Landmark Books

(2 days) ★

Tell students that tonight for homework you will be asking them to look for, and bring to school, a landmark book of their own. Suggest that today for independent reading, they look through the library for a familiar book. Students might find that your classroom library contains a landmark book that brings back special memories or feelings for them.

Independent Work Time

Give students the opportunity to look through the classroom library for familiar books before settling down for independent reading.

Home Connection

Tell students you would like to know what books are landmarks in their lives. Distribute a copy of *Letter to Parents* to each student. Tell them that for homework, they should find a book at home that is a landmark to them. Ask them to think and talk with their parents about why the book is a landmark for them. Remind them that they should come to school prepared to share.

Lesson 5
Landmark Books
(2 days) ★

Mini-Lesson (day 2)

Have students gather in the meeting area with their landmark books. Remind them of the conversation you had yesterday. Explain that today they will have an opportunity to share their landmark book and talk about why it is a landmark.

Encourage each student to present his or her book to the class. Ask questions such as:

- Why did you select this book to share?
- How often do you read this book?
- What is your favorite thing about this book?

Let other students ask questions, too.

Because you want to give each student an opportunity to share his or her book, your mini-lessons will be longer than usual. Depending on your class size, it may take two to three days. Make sure to leave some time each day for independent reading.

Independent Work Time

Invite students to share or trade their landmark books during independent reading time.

Home Connection

Have students interview someone from home about landmark books.

Share

Once all your students have shared their landmark books, create a chart with students' names and their landmark books. This chart can be posted in the hall or at the student bookstore.

Lesson 5
Landmark Books BLM 11
(2 days) ★

Dear Parent(s) or Guardian(s),

As you know, your child is learning about the importance of reading and sharing books with other readers. In our current lesson, we are talking about books that are important and special to us. They might be books that students have read so often they know them by heart. They could also be books that remind them of important times in their lives or a person who is very special to them. We call these books landmark books.

Help your child look through or remember some of the books that have been read or been read to her or him. Ask your child if any of them are landmark books. If your child doesn't have a landmark book, read one or two books aloud and ask her or him to choose one book to share at class tomorrow. When your child decides on a book to share, please have your child bring the book to school, or write the title and author of the book on a piece of paper.

We will be compiling a list of landmark books with the class. I will send the list home to you so you can read some of these books aloud to your child. Many of these landmark books will be available for your child to purchase in the student bookstore.

Thank you for helping make books a landmark in your child's life.

Sincerely,

Building a Community of Readers

Lesson 6
Books Are Special to Us
(2 days) ★

You will need:

- chart paper.
- one copy of *My Landmark Book* (BLM 12, page 33) for each child.
- a completed *My Landmark Book* prepared by you illustrating one of your landmark books.
- crayons, markers, or colored pencils for each child.

Lesson Objective

Lesson 6 continues to explore the importance of landmark books by summarizing the reasons why these books are important. Specifically in this lesson you will:

- help students brainstorm a list titled, *What special places do books hold in our lives?*
- have students illustrate and write about their landmark book.
- have the class share and discuss how books are special to them.

★ ★

Mini-Lesson (day 1)

Write *What special places do books hold in our lives?* on chart paper. Read the title and explain that together, the class will brainstorm a list of why books are landmarks in our lives. Remind students of the landmark book conversations you had in the previous lesson. Start the list by writing one or two of the reasons students selected their books. Ask students to help you add to the list. You may want to categorize your chart as shown on page 31.

Tell students that during independent reading time today, you want them to draw a picture illustrating the cover or a scene from their landmark book. Give students the handout titled *My Landmark Book*. Model the handout's use by sharing your own illustration. Tell them that they will only be working on the space for the picture today. Explain that tomorrow they will be working on adding words to their picture.

What special places do books hold in our lives?

Memories
- Remind us of special people
- Remind us of special places
- Remind us of special events

Entertainment
- Make us laugh
- Take us on adventures
- Take us to imaginary places

Learning and Growing
- Help us learn at school
- Teach us how to do things
- Teach us about new things
- Make us think

Bring Us Closer Together
- Make us see how others are like us, even when they are different
- Let us see how other people feel and think
- Give us something special to talk about

Independent Work Time

Students should work independently on their landmark illustrations. Circulate to support students who may be having difficulty.

Share

Have students bring their completed illustration to the meeting area. After they share their drawings, collect them. Tell students they will be given their illustrations back tomorrow when you will discuss adding words.

Mini-Lesson (day 2)

Remind students of their work yesterday. Tell them that today, they will add words to their picture. Ask students to look at the chart you made titled, *What special places do books hold in our lives?* Tell them that they will use this chart to help them add words to their picture.

Explain that you will be rereading the chart two times. The first time, you want them to listen to all the reasons listed and think about which reason most closely matches the reason their landmark book is special to them.

Before reading the chart the second time, tell students that this time you want them to raise their hand when you read the reason they thought most closely matched their own. As students raise their hands, have them come to the chart and put their initials next to the text.

Once all students have put their initials on the chart, explain that you want them to add words to the illustrations they worked on yesterday. Redistribute *My Landmark Book* to each student. Show students the lines and instruct them on writing the reason they selected their landmark book on the lines provided.

Independent Work Time

Students should work independently on adding words to their picture. Circulate to support students who may be having difficulty. When students have completed their worksheet, have them choose a book to read independently.

Share

After students share their finished sheets, collect their work. Use their work to create a bulletin board or a bound book to be displayed in your classroom library, school library, or student bookstore.

Lesson 6
Books Are Special to Us BLM 12
(2 days) ★

Name

My Landmark Book

▶ Lesson 7
Reading Recommendations
(2 days)★ ★

You will need:

- chalkboard or chart paper.
- 3–4 books you will recommend to the class.
- two copies of *My Book Recommendation* (BLM 13 and 14, pages 37 and 38) for each child.
- book bin labeled *Book Recommendations*.
- one copy of *Letter to Parents* (BLM 15, page 39) for each child.

Lesson Objective

In Lesson 7, students will learn that reading communities make book recommendations. Specifically in this lesson you will:

- discuss what the term *recommendation* means.
- show students how to make a book recommendation.
- create a class Reading Recommendations bin.

★ ★

Mini-Lesson (day 1)

Tell students that one way to make a strong reading community is to share ideas about books. Sharing the books you like and do not like, telling friends about authors you enjoy, or recommending a nonfiction book that will help with something they are working on are some of the ways readers share ideas about books.

Explain that a book recommendation is another way of saying, "Hey, I think you will like this book." Tell them that today, you will give them some book recommendations, show them how they can make their own recommendations, and introduce a special book bin your class will use to store the book recommendations.

Share with the class the books you have selected. Tell them they are all books you would like to recommend to the class. Share the title, author, and why you are recommending each book.

Once you have shared your book recommendations, ask students to think about a book they have read that they would like to recommend to a friend. Tell them that during independent reading, they should find that book and tell a friend about it. They may even decide to read their recommended book with a friend during this time.

©2005 Schoolwide, Inc. • **Unit 1** Building a Community of Readers • *Grades K-1*

Lesson 7
Reading Recommendations
(2 days) ★

Independent Work Time

As students read, conference as usual. If you notice students sharing recommendations, ask them about why they made their recommendation.

Share

Select a few students to share the book they recommended and why they recommended it. Tell them that tomorrow, you will show them a special place in the room where they will be able to put books they want to recommend as well as look for book others have recommended.

★ ★

▶ Teaching Tip

In preparation for modeling making book recommendations, be sure to have a variety of titles and reasons for making these recommendations. Recommendation possibilities include: a nonfiction book on a class pet, a book from a popular author, a book that is similar to one your students have already enjoyed, or a book about a topic your class has been talking about.

★ ★

Mini-Lesson (day 2)

Remind students of the conversation you had yesterday. Tell them that readers use recommendations to help them decide what to read. Explain that you have created a Recommended Reading bin for your reading community to use. Show students the bin and tell them where it will be located.

Explain that in addition to placing a book they recommend in the bin, when they want to make a book recommendation, there will be a special form for them to fill out. Show them the *My Book Recommendation* form and explain its use.

Distribute the *My Book Recommendation* form to each student. Tell students that they will all make a recommendation. Explain that the first step is to draw a picture that would tell another reader what the book is about.

Next, explain that a good book recommendation also tells a person how you feel about the book. Instruct students to color the face that depicts their feeling about the book and write a comment about it.

Finally, explain that a recommendation should also tell who they think would like to read the book. Instruct students to write about or draw a picture of the people they think would like to read it.

Show students where the blank forms will be stored for future use. Explain that completed book recommendation sheets will be kept in the Reading Recommendation bin so that if someone borrows a book from the bin, another reader can still read the recommendation.

Tell students that these sheets may also be copied and taken to the bookstore. The bookstore is a great place to share recommendations with students in the entire school community.

Independent Work Time

Conference as usual and support students who wish to fill out an additional reading recommendation form.

Share

Have students share a few of the recommendations to reinforce the proper usage and storage of them.

Home Connection

Send another copy of the *My Book Recommendation* form home with students along with the *Letter to Parents*. Explain to students that they should have a friend or family member read a book with them and complete another book recommendation. Tell students to bring their recommendations to school the next day to place in the Reading Recommendations bin.

Lesson 7
Reading Recommendations BLM 13
(2 days) ★

My Book Recommendation

Name:

Book title:

Author:

1. Draw a picture about this book.

My Book Recommendation

2. I thought this book was:

good.   okay.   bad.

3. These people would like this book.

Lesson 7
Reading Recommendations BLM 15
(2 days) ★

Dear Parent(s) or Guardian(s),

Today in class, we talked about how people find out about books that might interest them. One way is hearing a recommendation from a friend, classmate, or family member. Each student wrote a book recommendation for one of their landmark books. We then discussed their recommendations and placed them in a file for future reference. Throughout the year, we will add to this file so students will have a place to go to learn more about books they might like to read.

Tonight, please read a book with your child. Then, help your child complete the *My Book Recommendation* worksheets attached to this letter. Have your child bring the form, and if possible, the book, back to school the next day to share with the class. We will place your child's recommendation in our class file.

Don't forget to stop by the school with your child to browse through our student bookstore. Many of the books your child's classmates recommended are there. Once again, thank you for being a part of our community of readers.

Sincerely,

Building a Community of Readers

SCHOOLWIDE, INC.
LITERACY PROGRAMS

Lesson 8
Tools of Reading
(2 days) ★

You will need:

- markers, crayons, or colored pencils for each child.
- one copy of *Bookmark Template* (BLM 16, page 44) for each child.
- 10 double-sided copies of *My Reading Record* (BLM 17, page 45) stapled together with a blank cover for each child.
- one copy of *Letter to Parents* (BLM 18, page 46) for each child.
- light cardboard or poster paper for making bookmarks and covers.

Lesson Objective

Lesson 8 introduces students to a few of the tools that readers can use when reading. As students recognize the value of these tools, they will be more likely to take advantage of them. Specifically in this lesson you will:

- make a list of useful reading tools.
- help each child make a personalized bookmark.
- help students create their own reading record.

★ ★

Mini-Lesson (day 1)

Write *Useful Reading Tools* on the chalkboard or chart paper. Explain to the class that all readers use certain tools to make reading easier and more enjoyable. Ask the class to suggest useful items that would go on a list of tools for reading. Write their suggestions on the chalkboard or chart paper. Make sure that the list includes bookmarks and a record of books read. Tell students that after they brainstorm the list, you will help them make some of the reading tools for themselves. Your list may include the following on the chart to the right.

Useful Reading Tools

- Someone to read to you
- Good lighting
- A comfortable, quiet place to sit
- A bookmark to keep your place
- Tape-recorded stories to read along in books you can't read alone
- A partner who can help with parts you can't read
- A record of the books you've read to help you remember them

Lesson 8
Tools of Reading
(2 days) ★

Photocopy the *Bookmark Template* on heavy paper or paste copies of the template on cardboard. Cut out the bookmarks and distribute them to students. Explain that bookmarks are used to help readers keep their place in a book until they are ready to read it at another time.

Instruct the students to decorate their bookmarks using crayons, markers, and colored pencils. Suggest that students create a bookmark that will inspire them as readers. Model for students how to decorate a bookmark leaving a blank area for them to write their names.

Independent Work Time

Allow students ample time to create their personalized bookmarks. When students are finished, have them read independently and use the tool they created.

Share

Bring the class together to have students share their bookmark designs, and discuss how they used them if they had a chance to do so.

Home Connection

Send each child's bookmark home along with the *Letter to Parents* that explains this lesson.

▶ Teaching Tip

Additional bookmark templates can be placed in an accessible location for students to take and use throughout the year.

Lesson 8
Tools of Reading
(2 days) ★

Mini-Lesson (day 2)

Review the list of reading tools to see if students can think of any other tools to add to the list. Then, tell students that you will show them a new tool and explain how they will use it. Explain that this tool will help them remember all the books they have read and allow them to record and reflect on the different types and categories of books they read.

Distribute one copy of *My Reading Record* to each student. Model for students how the record is to be filled out by completing one for a book you previously shared with them. Go over the information in each column and explain what it means. After you have demonstrated it, give students the booklets containing blank record sheets. Tell them they will use these reading records at school and at home.

Independent Work Time

Students should read independently as usual. Provide time at the end of the independent reading session for students to fill in one box on the record sheet.

SCHOOLWIDE, INC.
LITERACY PROGRAMS

42

Lesson 8
Tools of Reading
(2 days) ★

Share

Have students share their completed reading records. Be sure to highlight its proper use.

Home Connection

Send the booklets home and tell students to illustrate the cover of their reading record booklet.

★ ★

▶ Teaching Tip

If you have your own reading record of books you have read, bring it in and share it with the class. If not, make one for yourself and share your entries with the class throughout the year.

SCHOOLWIDE, INC.
LITERACY PROGRAMS

★ ★

Bookmark Template

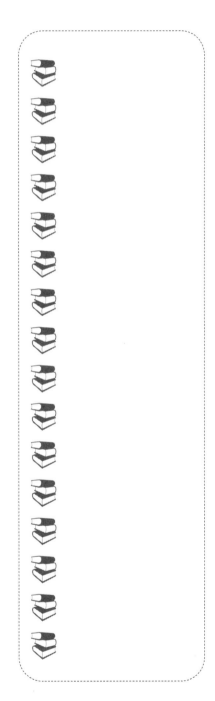

Lesson 8
Tools of Reading BLM 17
(2 days) ★

Dear Parent(s) or Guardian(s),

Our class is working on a lesson about the tools readers use. Today, your child made a bookmark. Take a look at the bookmark your child created and ask how he or she came up with the design. Praise your child for her or his efforts.

Choose a favorite book and read it to your child. At some point, pause and place the bookmark on the last page read and close the book. Discuss what has happened in the book so far with your child. Then, open the book and remove the bookmark, explaining how it kept your place in the book.

In a few days your child will bring home a Reading Record booklet that he or she created. Throughout the year, your child will write down each book he or she reads or has been read to at school and at home. The reading record has a place to record the author and title, the date the book was read, and what your child thinks about the book, for example, whether he or she liked it or whether he or she would want to read it again.

At least five days a week, please take 10 to 15 minutes to read a book to your child. After you read the book, write down the information about that book in his or her reading record. Praise your child for being a good reader, and tell him or her how much you enjoy reading together.

Be sure your child expresses an opinion about the book. It is fine if your child does not like a particular book and does not want to read it again. Not all books are right for every reader, and we all have personal tastes. Of course, it is wonderful news if your child likes a book so much that she or he wants to read it over and over and over again. Reading the same book repeatedly is another step on the road to independent reading.

Thank you so much for your help and being a part of our community of readers.

Sincerely,

Building a Community of Readers

SCHOOLWIDE, INC.
LITERACY PROGRAMS

My Reading Record

Name:

★ ★

Title: Date

Author:

★ ★

Title: Date

Author:

★ ★

Title: Date

Author:

Parent comments:

Lesson 9
The Value of Reading and Being a Member of a Reading Community
(3 days) ★

You will need:

- one copy of *The Bee Tree*, by Patricia Polacco.
- one copy of *The Wednesday Surprise*, by Eve Bunting.
- one copy of *Thank you, Mr. Falker*, by Patricia Polacco.
- chalkboard or chart paper.

Introduction

For the next three days, you will be reading books about reading and reading communities. You will talk about the characters and situations in the stories and use that information to help your class build a community of readers.

Lesson Objective

Lesson 9 introduces pupils to stories about characters whose lives are enriched by reading and being a part of a reading community. These books should lead students to consider the value of reading in their own lives. Specifically in this lesson you will:

- discuss the value of reading.
- read aloud three books to the class and discuss the stories.

★ ★

Mini-Lesson (days 1–3)

Before reading, tell students that over the next few days you will be reading aloud three special books about reading. Tell them you have selected these books because of all the work they have done so far to build a strong reading community. Explain that each character in the books you will read is a member of, or learns something about, a strong reading community.

Read one book each day. Tell students that after you read each book, you will talk about the characters and messages about reading that each book implies.

During each read-aloud, be sure to stop along the way to clarify meaning and check on comprehension.

Lesson 9

The Value of Reading and Being a Member of a Reading Community

(3 days) ★

The following is a list of some ideas gathered from the suggested titles:

• *The Bee Tree*—Communities work together to pass along the importance of reading. Communities celebrate reading and get excited for each other's reading achievements.

• *The Wednesday Surprise*—Sometimes reading is hard but if members of the community help each other, everyone can succeed. When reading is hard, ask another member of the community for help. You are never too young or old to be a member of a reading community.

• *Thank you, Mr. Falker*—All readers are different and learn in different ways. Sometimes reading is easy, sometimes reading is hard. Reading communities are supportive of each other. Patience and kindness are the best way to help each other become strong readers.

Independent Work Time

Have students read independently or with a partner. Carry the day's read-aloud book with you as you conference. Use the book to talk to students about their reading experiences and any connection they made to the character or story.

Share

As a final assessment of this unit, gather students in the meeting area, create a chart titled, *We Are a Community of Readers*. Show the cover of the book read that day and reiterate the message it teaches about reading and reading communities. Then, have the class brainstorm ways that they are a community of readers. List their responses on the chart.

★ ★

▶ Teaching Tip

These mini-lessons will be longer than most because you will be reading a book and discussing its content. If possible, provide two sessions for each book, allowing time to read the book in one session and time to talk about it in another.

unit 2
Book Choice & Independent Reading

★ ★

Introduction

As a teacher, you have the ability to excite children about reading and to expose them to the many different types of books available to read. You can also teach them about how to choose books that are appropriate for them. Many times, children will choose a book based solely on its cover illustration. You can teach students how to explore further and dig a little deeper when choosing books. In this unit, students will uncover the many ways that readers select books. They will share with each other how they make decisions, and they will learn how the adults in their lives make their book choices.

An important goal of this unit is for each of your students to become an informed reader. If students learn to look for clues as to what a book holds, they will feel empowered and responsible when choosing books. The lessons in Unit 2 will help you show your students how to make careful book choices by:

- learning to stay focussed and productive during independent reading time.
- thinking about how readers choose books.
- learning what a "just right book" is and how to find one.
- practicing finding a "just right book."
- discovering how books are organized in different places.
- recognizing the many different types of books to choose from and becoming more familiar with various book genres.
- reflecting on personal reading preferences.

Knowing how to select books for independent reading is an important life skill that not only helps readers when they are looking for information, but also informs them when they are making choices for pleasure reading. Sharing your knowledge about how to make careful and thoughtful decisions about books will travel with your children to all of the places that they choose books, from the Schoolwide Bookstore to libraries and bookstores they visit as adults.

Lesson 1
How Are We Staying Focused and Productive During Independent Reading Time?
(1 day) ★

You will need:

• one picture book.

Lesson Objective

In Lesson 1 students will review what to do during independent reading time and practice partner reading. Specifically in this lesson you will:

• review a list of practical rules and routines for independent reading time.
• demonstrate effective partner reading skills.

★ ★

Mini-Lesson

Introduce this lesson by telling students that today, you want to talk about independent reading time. Tell students it is important that the class maintain rules to follow during this time so that everyone can enjoy reading and work at becoming strong, independent readers. Review with students the chart *Rules for Independent Reading Time* created in Unit 1, Lesson 3.

Explain that sometimes readers choose to read by themselves, and other times, readers want to read together. Explain that one way readers can stay focussed and productive during independent reading time is to read with a partner.

Tell students that today, you want them to think about how good readers read together. Explain that one important way is to sit side-by-side so that both readers can see the book they are sharing. Ask students to think of other ways good readers read books together, e.g., by holding the book in the middle of the two readers, putting it on one person's lap, etc. After the discussion, model with a student good habits that readers do when they read together.

Lesson 1
How Are We Staying Focused and Productive During Independent Reading Time?
(1 day) ★

Independent Work Time

Encourage students to read with a partner and practice effective strategies for partner reading.

Share

Bring the class together and have them discuss how independent reading went and how they could make it better next time. Encourage those who read with a partner to share their experience.

★ ★

▶ Teaching Tip

Use this lesson to refocus students' attention on classroom management and productivity. Rereading the rules you created earlier in the year and adding to them is an excellent way to maintain a strong, independent reading time.

► Lesson 2
How Do Readers Choose Books?

(1 day) ★

You will need:

- chalkboard or chart paper.
- one copy of *Letter to Parents* (BLM 19, page 54) for each student.
- baskets or boxes of age-appropriate books.

Lesson Objective

Lesson 2 will make students more aware of the different reasons why readers choose particular books and teach them how to make more informed book choices. Specifically in this lesson you will:

- discuss the reasons why people choose certain books.
- help students choose a book.
- encourage students to share their book choices with classmates and families.

★ ★

Mini-Lesson

Ask students to name the places they go to choose books, for example the student bookstore, school library, public library, classroom library, home, etc. Next, ask them to think about how they pick books. List their responses on chart paper under the heading, *Ways We Choose Books*. Responses might include the illustrations, author, content, title, a recommendation, a movie tie-in, part of a series, etc. Help students brainstorm ways readers make decisions about book selections. Save this list to use again in Lessons 3 and 12.

Ways We Choose Books

- To learn more about a topic
- Because we like the author
- Because the illustrations are interesting
- The cover looked very interesting
- A friend recommended it
- Because it is about something I am interested in
- I could relate to the story or topic
- It is a book I have read before

Lesson 2
How Do Readers Choose Books?
(1 day) ★

Independent Work Time

Let students browse through the baskets of books set on tables and choose one they would like to read. Be sure there are a good variety of topics, authors, and genre such as fiction, nonfiction, poetry, and picture books. Students may spend the entire independent work time browsing, or they may begin reading one book. Circulate around the room to support students and assess the ways in which they are making their book choices.

Share

Invite students to sit in a circle with their books. First, share your observations with the class. Praise those individuals who went beyond the cover to look inside the book and skim parts of it. Next, tell students they will take turns holding up their books and explaining why they picked it. As students do this, make connections between their reasons, e.g. "Greg and Akim both chose books about sports heroes. They are both interested in that topic." Add new ideas to the list you created earlier, e.g. "Chelsea chose a book about tennis because she wanted to learn more about it."

Home Connection

Send home with students the *Letter to Parents* that explains this lesson.

★ ★

▶ Teaching Tip

Observe how students are handling books. Do they skim through the pages or just look at the cover? Notice what they do when they narrow down their choices, i.e. do they read the first page or other pages in the book? Walk around the room and check in with individuals to ask about their book selection. Use the information you gather to start the Share discussion.

Lesson 2
How Do Readers Choose Books? BLM 19
(1 day) ★

Dear Parent(s) or Guardian(s),

One of my goals this year in reading is to help your child become a lifelong reader. To this end, we will be studying not just the skills of reading but reading behaviors. Today we began a study of how readers choose books. A list of ideas we discussed is in the chart below.

One way you can support your child in developing positive reading behaviors is by talking to him or her about books. Share with your child the reading you do and the decisions you make about what and when to read.

Ways We Choose Books

- To learn more about a topic
- Because we like the author
- Because the illustrations are interesting
- The cover looked very interesting
- A friend recommended it
- Because it is about something I am interested in
- I could relate to the story or topic
- It is a book I have read before

The student bookstore is a great place to support your child in making smart book choices and finding out about his or her selection process. The next time you and your child visit the student bookstore, browse through the books and talk with your child about his or her interests. Use the information in our chart to help your child find a book that is just right. Reinforcing the work we are doing in class will help your child develop positive reading behaviors that will last a lifetime.

Thank you for your help in allowing your child to explore the ways to unlock the treasures found in books.

Sincerely,

Building a Community of Readers

Lesson 3
Choosing a "Just Right Book"
(1 day) ★

You will need:
- chalkboard or chart paper.
- the list of "Ways We Choose Books" created in Lesson 1 of this unit.
- a collection of children's books in a variety of genre.
- boxes or baskets of books for students to browse through.
- a prepared chart: *What are "Just Right Books"?*.

Lesson Objective

Lesson 3 will teach your students to select books that they can work with for a sustained period of time. Students will learn that a "just right book" is one that can help them learn and strengthen their reading skills. Specifically in this lesson you will:

- model appropriate book choices for kindergarten and first-grade readers.
- model how readers monitor for comprehension.

★ ★

Mini-Lesson

Show students the list of *Ways We Choose Books* created in Lesson 2. Review the various ways that readers choose books and ask if they have thought of any others to add to the list. Then, introduce the concept of choosing a "just right book." Explain that, for kindergarten or first-grade readers, a "just right book" is a book that they can spend a lot of time with and can use to help them become better readers.

Model by sharing books that provide students with a variety of explanations of what a "just right book" can be. For example, choose a nonfiction book about a class pet, or other topic of interest to your class to show how a "just right book" can help the reader learn about a topic. Select a poem you have read aloud and enjoyed often with your class to model how a "just right book" can be a poem they have heard and want to reread. You might also share a well-known fairy tale to model how a "just right book" can be a story you know well and want to retell.

SCHOOLWIDE, INC.
LITERACY PROGRAMS

Lesson 3
Choosing a "Just Right Book"

(1 day) ★

After you have shared your collection of books, show students the chart titled, *What are "Just Right Books"?*. Read aloud each of the bullets and answer any questions students might have.

Invite students to look through the book bins and select three "just right books" to read during independent reading time. Save this chart to use in Lesson 6.

What Are "Just Right Books"?

- Nonfiction books with a lot of pictures and captions that will help me learn about an interesting topic
- Books I have already read or heard and can reread
- Fairy tale books that I know and can retell
- Alphabet books that can help me learn letters and new words
- Books that I can read the words and understand
- Books that have pictures and only a few words on each page
- Wordless picture books

Independent Work Time

During independent reading, check to see which books students think are just right for them. Circulate around the room to monitor the conversations of students as they choose their books. Ask questions to help you understand how they are making their choices. You will use this information as a starting point for the Share discussion.

Share

Have some of the students share their book choices. Point out why the students' book choices were "just right" ones. Tell students that in the future during independent reading, you will expect them to be thoughtful about choosing just right books.

Lesson 4
Shopping for Books
(1 day) ★

You will need:

- book baggies for each student.
- a selection of books from your reading—for example, a novel, teacher's manual, newspaper, or magazine.

Lesson Objective

Lesson 4 will give your students an opportunity to apply what they learned about book selection in Lessons 2 and 3 of this unit. They will browse through the classroom library to choose books they will hold onto and read during independent reading for one week. Specifically in this lesson you will:

- reinforce book-selecting skills.
- review the reasons why readers choose certain books.

★ ★

Mini-Lesson

Have students review the *What are "Just Right Books"?* chart you discussed in Lesson 3.

Tell students that good readers always have a collection of books ready. Explain that good readers do this because they want to spend as much time reading as they can. Share with students your collection of books and tell them that you keep them on-hand at your reading spot such as, a bedside table, shoulder bag, coffee table, etc. Whenever you have time to read, your books are right there waiting for you.

Tell students that because they are good readers, you would like to give them book baggies. In their book baggies they will keep a collection of books. They will go shopping in the classroom library for books to put in their baggie each week.

Explain to your students that they will be keeping the books they select for one week. Because of this, tell them they will need to think carefully about the books they choose. Tell students they should select their books from the classroom library using all the book selection skills they have learned so far.

Lesson 4
Shopping for Books
(1 day) ★

Independent Work Time

Hand out the book baggies to each student. Tell them to choose books from the classroom library and place them in the baggies. Reinforce that these will be the books that they will read during independent reading time this week.

Kindergarten and first-grade students should select approximately six books for their book baggies. It is a good idea to suggest that they select a few books from each of the categories in the *What Are Just Right Books?* chart.

Share

Bring the class together to talk about the books in their baggies. Ask question about their choices and reinforce good book selection decisions.

★ ★

▶ Teaching Tip

Having students keep book baggies is a great way to cut down traffic during independent reading time and reinforce positive book-selecting behaviors. Assign a book-shopping day each week for selecting and returning books to the classroom library. Tell students that you expect them to make smart choices because, except for special circumstances, the classroom library will only be open for shopping on the designated day.

Conference with students during independent reading time to confirm and support their book choices. If necessary bring them into the library to select new or additional books.

Lesson 5
Choosing a Reading Nook
(1 day) ★

You will need:

- chalkboard or chart paper.
- one copy of *My Reading Nook* (BLM 20 and 21, page 61 and 62) for each child.

Lesson Objective

This classroom management lesson will help your students reflect on the best environment for independent reading. As you begin to reinforce book-choice and reading for sustained periods of time, the classroom environment becomes extremely important. The proper reading environment is one in which there are little or no distractions, students are staying in one place, and there are no superfluous noises, i.e. pencil sharpeners, bathroom breaks, non-reading talk. If your classroom reading environment is already like this, you may decide to skip this lesson. If not, "Choosing a Reading Nook" should help. Specifically in this lesson you will:

- list the characteristics that make a place good for reading.
- identify the spots around the room where students can independently read.
- help students complete the *My Reading Nook* worksheet.

★ ★

Mini-Lesson

Tell students you have noticed that during independent reading some of them have found great reading places that work for them. They look comfortable, productive, and they stay in one place during the entire time. Ask students if they have ever heard of the term *reading nook*. Explain that a reading nook is a spot that helps readers focus and allows them to get lots of reading done. Have students brainstorm the conditions that make a good reading nook at home or at the library, i.e. quiet, well-lit, and comfortable. Chart their responses on the chalkboard or chart paper.

Tell students to think about the place(s) they read each day. Does it work for them? Is it a spot where they can focus and read? Before sending them off to independent reading time, ask students to decide if the place they read is a perfect nook for them or if they need to find a new place that will help them get the most out of their independent reading time.

Lesson 5
Choosing a Reading Nook
(1 day) ★

Independent Work Time

Your main objective in teaching this lesson is to support students who are often distracted or not productive during independent reading. As students read independently, watch for the choices they make. Assist those students who have not previously found a space that works well for them.

Share

Call the students together to share their reading nooks. Ask them why they chose their spot and whether or not it worked for them. Discuss ways in which you can work to make your classroom one big reading nook. Here are some ideas:

- Keep the classroom very quiet.
- Don't move around the room.
- Bring in reading pillows for the library area.
- Stay away from friends or people who distract you.
- Have a special reading light that we only turn on during reading time.
- Keep reading places neat and organized.

Tell students that tonight for homework, they will draw and write about a reading nook at home. Explain that you will use their writings and drawings to come up with more ideas for the classroom.

Home Connection

Ask students to think about the places in their home that are perfect for reading. Hand out the *My Reading Nook* worksheet and instruct students how to complete it. Have students take their worksheets home. Tell them to share them with their parents and bring them back to school the next day.

★ ★

▶ Teaching Tip

Highlight students who have already been making smart choices during independent reading time and already have a reading nook. Their nook may be at their desk or on the rug in the meeting area. Ask them to share why they choose to read there and how it works for them.

　　　　©2005 Schoolwide, Inc. • **Unit 2** Book Choice and Independent Reading • *Grades*

Lesson 5
Choosing a Reading Nook BLM 20
(1 day) ★

Name:

My Reading Nook
What is the best place at home for reading? Describe it and tell why and when you like to read there.

1. My reading nook at home is:

2. I like this spot because:

3. The time that is the best to read there is:

because:

Name:

My Reading Nook (cont.)

4. Draw a picture of you reading in your reading nook at home.

Lesson 6
Ways to Organize Books

(2 days) ★

You will need:

- books from the classroom library.
- baskets or boxes affixed with labeled and unlabeled index cards.
- chart *What Are "Just Right Books"?* from Lesson 3.
- sticky notes.

Lesson Objective

Lesson 6 will provide students the opportunity to further explore the many types of books available to read and the many ways that books can be organized. It will also help create a structure in your classroom that will support book choice. Specifically in this lesson students will:

- talk about ways books can be organized.
- organize the classroom library into categories of books.
- discuss why they organized the classroom library in the way they did.

★ ★

Mini-Lesson (day 1)

The library, local bookstore, or school bookstore are a few of the places readers go to select books. Tell students that in all these places the books are organized in ways that help readers make good book choices. In the library for example, the school librarian groups nonfiction books according to the Dewey Decimal system. This system is a way to organize books by topic. The librarian may also sort books according to themes or topics that are being taught at school at that time.

Tell students that because the class is working hard at making good book choices, it makes sense to organize the classroom library in ways that will be helpful. Refer the class to the chart, *What are "Just Right Books"?*. Explain to students that they will use this chart to help them organize the classroom library.

What Are "Just Right Books"?

- Nonfiction books with a lot of pictures and captions that will help me learn about an interesting topic
- Books I have already read or heard and can reread
- Fairy tale books that I know and can retell
- Alphabet books that can help me learn letters and new words
- Books that I can read words of and understand
- Books that have pictures and only a few words on each page
- Wordless picture books

SCHOOLWIDE, INC.
LITERACY PROGRAMS

▶ Lesson 6
Ways to Organize Books
(2 days)★ ★

Show students the baskets with affixed labels. Read each of the labels and explain that today, you want them to look through all the books in the library and sort them according to the labeled baskets. Explain that there will be some books that do not match the labels you have created. Show students the baskets with blank labels and tell them that when they come across a book that doesn't match they should place that book in a blank-labeled basket.

Demonstrate the process for students by randomly selecting six books from your library. Think out-loud as you determine in which basket it should be placed.

Once you have demonstrated the process, tell students that they will be working with a partner to sort books and that before a book is placed in a basket, both partners should agree on its placement. Confirm that students understand your expectation.

Independent Work Time

Tell students you want each partnership to select 10 books from the classroom library. Explain that they should talk about the 10 books they select and decide where they will be placed. Once students have a collection of books, tell them to find a place to spread out and begin their discussions. When they have decided, they should put a sticky note on each book with a letter or word that will help them remember the basket in which they want it to go.

Explain that the books will not actually be placed in the baskets until Share time. Circulate to support students in deciding and posting their books.

Share

Ask students to sit in a big circle. Place all the labeled baskets and two blank-labeled baskets in the center of the circle. Pair-by-pair, ask students to share their books and their decision about where it should be placed. Once their decision is agreed upon by the class, have students remove the sticky note and place each book in the correct basket.

Once all the books are placed in baskets, set the baskets in the classroom library for use. Set aside books in blank-labeled baskets, and tell students you will begin thinking about these books tomorrow.

©2005 Schoolwide, Inc. • **Unit 2** Book Choice and Independent Reading • *Grades K-1*

Lesson 6
Ways to Organize Books

(2 days)★ ★

Mini-Lesson (day 2)

Gather students in a circle in the meeting area. Spread out a large collection of the books that were in blank-labeled baskets. Remind students of the work they did yesterday and compliment them on it. Tell them that today you want to think about the books that did not fit any category and think of ways those books can be organized. Ask students to look at the covers and think about ways they could categorize these books. On a piece of chart paper write the title *Possible Book Baskets*. Gather students' ideas and record them on the chart.

Possible Book Baskets

- Funny books
- Sad books
- Books about animals
- Favorite books
- Books about people
- Books by favorite authors
- Books by favorite illustrators
- Books about places

From your list of possible ideas have the class vote on which are best for your classroom library. Write the determined label on the blank-labeled baskets. Assign groups of four students to each newly-labeled basket and tell them that during independent reading time, their job will be to look through the books that have not already been placed and find the ones that fit their basket.

Independent Work Time

As students look through books, support them by asking them to look beyond the cover and explain their decisions. This is a messy endeavor and that is okay. As long as students are looking, talking, and making decisions about books, the goals of this lesson are being achieved.

Share

Gather students together in the meeting area with their baskets. Have them share some of the books in the basket and tell about the process. After each group has shared their basket, determine where in the library each basket will be placed. Once all groups have shared, remind students of all their hard work in organizing the library and stress the importance of maintaining your newly organized library.

★ ★

▶ Teaching Tip

Depending on your class size and the size of your classroom library, this lesson my take more than one day. However, is not necessary for students to go through every book in your library at once. This can be an ongoing process and one that you adjust throughout the year.

Your objective is to have students get to know the books in the classroom library and to reinforce their notion of "just right books." Don't worry about whether their decisions about book placement are "correct." The important thing is that they are looking through books, thinking, and making decisions about them.

Students may find that some books match more than one category and therefore, have trouble deciding in which basket it should be placed. Knowing where the book is placed is not as important as the conversation about it. You can act as a mediator. Creating an undecided basket and reading these books aloud at a later date is one way to get students thinking more critically about them.

Lesson 7
Introducing Genres: Fables and Fairy Tales

(1 day) ★

You will need:

- chart paper.
- a basket or box of books which contains fables and fairy tales.

Lesson Objective

Lessons 7 through 11 will introduce your students to a variety of literary genres. The purpose of these lessons is to expose students to genres they may not be aware of but might want to try in the future.

Lesson 7 introduces fables and fairy tales. Students will hear fables and fairy tales read aloud and will discuss common characteristics of each. They will have an opportunity to independently read a selection of fables and fairy tales and look for these characteristics. Specifically in this lesson you will:

- outline the characteristics of fables and fairy tales.
- encourage students to read fables and fairy tales.

★ ★

Mini-Lesson

Tell students that one way readers choose books is by genre. Explain that the term *genre* means "a category or type of literature." Write the heading, *Readers Choose Books by Genre*, on chart paper. Under it, write the sub-headings, *Fables* and *Fairy Tales*. First ask students to share what they know about the characteristics of fables and fairy tales. List the characteristics.

Show students the basket that has been created for books with fables and fairy tales. Show them where these books will be stored in the classroom library. If students would like to add a fairy tale or fable to their book baggie, allow them to do so.

Readers Choose Books
by Genre

Fables and Fairy Tales

- Animals are often main characters of the story
- There is often a mischievous or "bad" character
- Stories often teach a lesson
- Sometimes something magical happens

Lesson 7
Introducing Genres: Fables and Fairy Tales
(1 day) ★

Independent Work Time

Students should read independently as usual. Conference with students who have selected to read a fairy tale or fable. Discuss how knowing the genre's characteristics helps readers understand the story.

Share

After independent reading time, bring the class together to discuss the books they read. Point out those students who read fables and fairy tales. Ask how they liked the stories and invite them to give recommendations.

★ ★

▶ Teaching Tip

Have small groups of students create genre posters that explain the features of fables and fairy tales. Encourage students to illustrate some of the characters and scenes from the fables and fairy tales that they read. Display the posters in the Schoolwide Bookstore.

Lesson 8
Introducing Genres: Nonfiction
(1 day) ★

You will need:

- chart paper.
- the list of genre characteristics from lesson 7.
- a basket or box of nonfiction books.

Lesson Objective

Lesson 8 will introduce the genre of nonfiction to your students. Students will learn what nonfiction books are and how they are usually written. They will be provided an opportunity to read a nonfiction book and share what they learned about the topic. Specifically in this lesson you will:

- explain the difference between fiction and nonfiction.
- explain some features of nonfiction books.
- encourage students to read a nonfiction book.

★ ★

Mini-Lesson

Re-introduce the term genre as a category or type of literature. Refer to the heading, *Readers Choose Books by Genre*, on the chart paper from Lesson 7. Point to the sub-heading, *Fables and Fairy Tales* and tell students that they will explore another kind of genre called nonfiction. Write *Nonfiction* as a sub-heading on chart paper and hang it next to the *Fairy Tales* chart.

Tell students that a fictional story is one that is made up. It is about imaginary people and happenings. Nonfiction is writing about the real world, real people, or true events. Discuss some of the characteristics of nonfiction and list them under the sub-heading *Nonfiction*. Ask students what types of nonfiction they have read. Biographies, information books, reference books, how-to books, and articles are possible responses.

Show students the basket or baskets created for nonfiction books and showthem where these books will be stored in theclassroom library. If students would like to adda nonfiction book to their book baggie, allow them to do so.

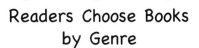

Readers Choose Books by Genre

Nonfiction

- Contains truthful information
- Can contain photographs, maps, diagrams, and other visual aids
- Can contain different size print
- Sometimes contains captions

SCHOOLWIDE, INC.
LITERACY PROGRAMS

Introducing Genres: Nonfiction

(1 day) ★

Independent Work Time

Students should read independently as usual. Conference with students who have selected to read nonfiction. Discuss how knowing the genre's characteristics helps readers understand the topic.

Share

After independent reading time, bring the class together to discuss the books they read. Point out those students who read nonfiction books. Ask how they liked the books and invite them to give recommendations.

★ ★

▶ Teaching Tip

Have small groups of students create genre posters that explain the features of nonfiction books. Encourage students to illustrate some of the information from the nonfiction books that they read. Display the posters in the Schoolwide Bookstore.

▶ Teaching Tip

If time permits, explain to students that nonfiction books have many features that fiction books do not. Hold up a nonfiction book and point to features such as the table of contents, index, glossary, photos and captions, diagrams, subheads, etc.

Lesson 9
Introducing Genres: Mysteries
(1 day) ★

You will need:

• chart paper.
• the list of genre characteristics from lessons 7 and 8.
• a basket or box of mystery books.

Lesson Objective

Lesson 9 will introduce the genre of mysteries to your students. Students will discuss some common characteristics of mysteries. They will be given an opportunity to read a mystery book and look for these characteristics. Specifically in this lesson you will:

• outline the characteristics that make up a mystery.
• show students where to find mystery books in the library.

★ ★

Mini-Lesson

Refer to the heading, *Readers Choose Books by Genre*, on the chart paper from Lessons 7 and 8 and review the meaning of fables, fairy tales, and nonfiction. Tell students that they will explore another kind of genre called mysteries. Write *Mysteries* as a sub-heading. Explain that a mystery is one kind of fictional story. Ask students to name some mystery books they've read or mystery TV shows or movies they have seen. Invite students to brainstorm the characteristics that these books have in common, and list these characteristics on the chart.

Show students the basket that has been created for mystery books and show them where these books will be stored in the classroom library. If students would like to add a mystery book to their book baggie, allow them to do so.

Readers Choose Books by Genre

Mysteries

• There is a problem that needs to be resolved.

• The main character always solves the problem by the end of the book.

• The chapters often end with cliff-hangers.

• There are clues throughout the story that often help the reader predict what will happen.

Independent Work Time

Students should read independently as usual. Conference with students who have selected to read mystery books. Discuss how knowing the genre's characteristics helps readers understand the story.

Share

After independent reading time, bring the class together to discuss the books they read. Point out those students who read mystery books. Ask how they liked the books and invite them to give recommendations.

★ ★

▶ Teaching Tip

Have small groups of students create genre posters that explain the features of mystery books. Encourage students to illustrate some of the events, characters, and scenes from the story that they read. Display the posters in the Schoolwide Bookstore.

Lesson 10
Introducing Genres: Realistic Fiction
(1 day) ★

You will need:

- chart paper.
- the list of genre characteristics from lessons 7, 8, and 9.
- a basket or box of realistic fiction books.

Lesson Objective

Lesson 10 will introduce the genre of realistic fiction to your students. Students will discuss some common characteristics of realistic fiction. They will be given an opportunity to read a realistic fiction book and look for these characteristics. Specifically in this lesson you will:

- outline the characteristics that make up realistic fiction.
- show students where to find realistic fiction books in the library.

★ ★

Mini-Lesson

Tell students that they will explore another kind of genre called realistic fiction. Write *Realistic Fiction* as a sub-heading on your genre chart. Explain that realistic fiction is a made-up story but that it can contain people, places, or events that seem real. It is similar to nonfiction in that some things may be real or true, but the story is fiction because it is imaginary or made up. Ask students to brainstorm books that they think would fall under this definition.

Show students the basket that has been created for realistic fiction books. Show them where these books will be stored in the classroom library. If students would like to add a realistic fiction book to their book baggie, allow them to do so.

Readers Choose Books by Genre

Realistic Fiction

- There are characters that the reader can relate to.
- The story seems like it could really happen.
- There are people, places, or events in the story that seem real.

▶ Lesson 10
Introducing Genres: Realistic Fiction
(1 day) ★

Independent Work Time

Students should read independently as usual. Conference with students who have selected to read realistic fiction books. Discuss how knowing the genre's characteristics helps readers understand the story.

Share

After independent reading time, bring the class together to discuss the books they read. Point out those students who read realistic fiction books. Ask how they liked the books and invite them to give recommendations.

★ ★

▶ Teaching Tip

Have small groups of students create genre posters that explain the features of realistic fiction books. Encourage students to illustrate some of the events, characters, and scenes from the story that they read. Display the posters in the Schoolwide Bookstore.

Lesson 11
Introducing Genres: Poetry
(1 day) ★

You will need:

- chart paper.
- the list of genre characteristics from lessons 7, 8, 9, and 10.
- a basket or box of poetry books or copies of poems.

Lesson Objective

Lesson 11 will introduce the genre of poetry to your students. Students will learn some common characteristics of this genre. They will have an opportunity to choose poems to read and look for these characteristics. Specifically in this lesson you will:

- outline the characteristics that make up poetry.
- share some poems and show where they can be found.

★ ★

Mini-Lesson

Tell students that they will explore another kind of genre called poetry. Write *Poetry* as a sub-heading on your genre chart. Read aloud poems that contain a variety of characteristics. Be sure to read non-rhyming poems as well as ones that rhyme. Ask students to help you list some of the characteristics of poetry. List these characteristics on the chart.

Show students the basket that has been created for poetry and show them where they will be stored in the classroom library. If students would like to add poems to their book baggies, allow them to do so.

Readers Choose Books by Genre

Poetry

- Words don't go all the way across the page in poems.
- Words are sometimes in different shapes, colors, or sizes in poems.
- Poems are sometimes short.
- Some poems rhyme or have rhythm.
- Poems sometimes contain interesting and vivid descriptions.

Independent Work Time

Students should read independently as usual. Conference with students who have selected to read poetry. Discuss how knowing the genre's characteristics helps readers understand the meaning of the poem.

Share at School

After independent reading time, bring the class together to discuss the books they read. Point out those students who read poetry. Ask how they liked the poems and invite them to give recommendations.

★ ★

▶ Teaching Tip

Have small groups of students create genre posters that explain the features of the poetry. Encourage students to illustrate some of the characters and scenes from the poems that they read. Display the posters in the Schoolwide Bookstore.

Lesson 12
Using What We Know: Shopping at the Bookstore
(1 day) ★

You will need:

- book baggies for each student.
- *Ways We Choose Books* list created in Lesson 2 of this unit.
- one copy of the *My Book Selection* (BLM 22, page 79) for each child.
- one copy of *Letter to Parents* (BLM 23, page 80) for each child.

Lesson Objective

Lesson 12 will give your students an opportunity to apply what they learned about book selection in Lessons 1 through 11. It will also give you a way to assess each student's progress in making good book selection decisions. Students will browse through the Schoolwide Bookstore to choose a book that they can independently read. Specifically in this lesson you will:

- reinforce book-selecting skills.
- review the reasons why readers choose certain books.
- help students complete the *My Book Selection* worksheet.

★ ★

Mini-Lesson

Remind students of all the work they have done since the beginning of this unit on book choice. Tell students that before moving on, you want to give them the opportunity to use what they have learned to select some books from the school bookstore.

Hand out the *My Book Selection* worksheet to students and tell them that they will be visiting the school bookstore during independent reading and you want them to use this sheet as they look through and select some books.

Clarify the terms on the worksheet and explain its use. Tell students that although they will not be buying books today, they should fill in their chart for possible future purchasing.

Independent Work Time

Take students to the Schoolwide Bookstore to browse through the books. Be sure to give students plenty of time to look through books and make good choices.

Lesson 11
Using What We Know: Shopping at the Bookstore
(1 day) ★

Share

After independent reading time, bring the class together to discuss the book selecting process and share new titles.

Home Connection

Have students take their checklist home. Invite them to share their book selecting experience with family members.

★ ★

▶ Teaching Tip

Walk around the bookstore and monitor students' choices. Encourage them to refer to the checklist as they are making their final choices. If time permits, allow students to take another tour of the bookstore with a partner to brainstorm the ways that the books are arranged and organized.

Lesson 11
Using What We Know: Shopping at the Bookstore BLM 22
(1 day) ★

Name:

My Book Selection

Title:

I selected this book because...

★ ★

Title:

I selected this book because...

★ ★

Title:

I selected this book because...

SCHOOLWIDE, INC.
LITERACY PROGRAMS

Building a Community of Readers

Dear Parent(s) or Guardian(s),

Over the past several weeks, our class has been discussing how to choose books that are interesting and appropriate for each individual student. We discussed the ways readers choose books and how each of us can choose a "just right book." Then, we practiced choosing appropriate books. An appropriate book for your child is one that she or he can read smoothly and with expression. It is one that your child understands and can retell to you. It is not too easy, though. It should present a challenge for your child in that she or he may pause briefly to sound out an unknown word or check for understanding. Most importantly, a "just right book" is one your child enjoys.

We also discussed how to organize our classroom library and manage our independent reading time. I gave book baggies to each student. At the beginning of each week, students chose several books from our classroom library to read during independent reading time. Students stored these books in their book baggies. In addition, we brainstormed and agreed to rules and routines for the class during independent reading time. I couldn't be more pleased with the progress the class has made.

Today, we went to the student bookstore and your child chose a book. As your child browsed through the books, he or she completed the attached worksheet. This worksheet helped remind your child what a "just right book" is. Review this worksheet with your child and ask why she or he chose this book. Discuss what makes a "just right book" for both your child and for yourself.

Today, we went to the student bookstore and your child practiced choosing a book. As your child browsed through the books, he or she completed the attached worksheet. Discuss with your child his or her book selections.

If you would like to send in money to purchase the book, or visit the bookstore with your child, please do so.

Thank you again for helping me bring the joy of reading to your child.

Sincerely,